IMPERFECT 10

A Practical Guide To Transform Your
Troubles Into Triumphs

MAXINE HABER

ISBN: 0998770787
ISBN-13: 978-0998770789 (Clarity Cove Publishing)

DEDICATION

To my mother, Fionie Cicely Smith Hinds. Thank you for being my Mommy, my mentor and my strength.

CONTENTS

ACKNOWLEDGMENTS

Thank you first and foremost to my family: my parents, Fionie Hinds and Maxwell Hinds, my sisters Sonya Washington and Nancy Hinds for being my first friends, my daughters Jennifer and Jacqueline Haber for being Mommy's cheering section and especially my best friend and #1 fan, my husband, Joseph Haber – thank you for being an integral part of my story for nearly 25 years. You have put up with all my craziness in the process of getting this book together. Thank you for supporting me as the photographer for my book cover and for being my personal graphic artist in designing the book jacket. I love you!

To my spectacular Vegas Besties: Jennifer Williams and Bianca Cummins, thank you for being my sisters, my inner circle and for loving me as I am. Kiosha Allen, Yessika Gamboa, Elaine Dowling, Kathleen Taylor, Dr. Monica Bickerstaff and Kim Bullock-Hennix: I appreciate the time you all have invested in me and making me feel like my voice was valued. To my Las Vegas Mommy crew – Lisa Romero, Andrea Accardi, Lauren Salazar, Erika Novak, Erica George, Trish Salomon, Rissa Stevens, Ariel Hailey and Cecilia Barba – I am so blessed to have such a generous, kind and sweet support network of women to be able to call my friends.

My South Florida friends: Rachel, Dan and the whole Nachman/Krimsky family, Ana, Robert and Savannah Anselmo, Dru Vega aka Lady D, Bobby Antoine, Sean Cruz-Smith, Councilman Scott Galvin, Jeff Stay and Jenny Stay and my brother from another mother Jeff Crean aka Sexy Johnny Walker.

Most of all, a special thank you to Nicolya Williams. Your guidance, instruction and kind words of encouragement have been nothing short of amazing. You believed in my book so much that you gave me the strength and confidence to believe in it too.

INTRODUCTION

This is not your typical self-help book and I am not the typical motivational author. Motivation is defined as follows: "External factors that stimulate desire and energy." This simply means that motivation comes from a source outside of yourself. The problem here is this: once the motivation is gone, the desire and energy go with it, leaving the once-motivated person in a state of inertia and frustration. The purpose of this book is NOT to just motivate you, but to change the negative perception you have of your circumstances and encourage you to believe in your ability to create positive change in your life, regardless of external forces (i.e. negative people, negative situations) and to give you the tools to create change along with the plan to make it happen. The word encourage originates from the French word "encoragier", which means "to strengthen". You know that you already have what it takes to transform your life, the purpose of this book is to shine a light on your ability, show you a path out of the darkness and strengthen that which is already inside of you. You will be empowered to grow your life in the direction you desire and embrace your imperfections. By embracing your imperfections, you will eliminate any power it has to hold you back, whatever you perceive your imperfections to be. One incredible example of this comes from the famous 'rap battle' scene in the hit movie "8 Mile" where Eminem's character, Rabbit, destroys his final adversary once and for all by embracing all of his perceived imperfections and verbally putting each one on display in front of everyone in the room. Every negative, each weakness, all of the "imperfections" that Rabbit knew his opponent could possibly use against him were rendered powerless the moment that he "owned" them. Throughout these pages you will find the tools you will use to transform your thoughts and behaviors, allowing you to move beyond your circumstances and get from your current space of just getting through life to truly living.

HOW TO READ IMPERFECT 10

To get the most out of reading Imperfect 10, I encourage you to read each chapter in order instead of just skipping around. Each chapter begins with an introduction to the chapter topic, followed by a personal story from my own life and the particular actions I took to overcome the obstacles I encountered. The chapters end with a special REALITY CHECK section that is designed to help you take the lessons from life and apply them to your own particular situation. As an **added bonus** to get you started, at the end of each chapter you will find an opportunity to put what you've learned into action with my "Ready, Set, Go" principle. Envision yourself for a moment as an athlete running a race. See the weeks and months you've put into training for this race. Now, envision yourself as standing in position on the starting line amongst your competition. Your hands are in place on the starting line, the track is laid out ahead to provide you with an exact path to head down, then BANG the starting pistol is shot to signal the race has begun. Yet, instead of taking off alongside the other athletes you simply stand around yelling "I am ready! I am SO ready!" Do you see the confusion on the faces of the crowd? Imagine your own eventual frustration at being ready and not taking any action to run your race. You can avoid being in this position right now by answering the "Ready, Set, Go" questions found at the end of each chapter in this book. These questions are designed to help you get clear about your imperfections, identify the **Functional Phrases** that can change your current mindset and help you decide which course of action to take. Instead of saying 'mantras' or even the popularized term 'affirmations', I chose to create the term **Functional Phrases** because then the words you use have purpose. Functional Phrases are **"Words That Work"**. You can go back and review your answers as you move forward through this book. Be clear and honest, the answers are for you and no one else. It is my goal with Imperfect 10 to share my story and give you the specific actions you can take to overcome similar obstacles and begin truly living the life of your dreams. Even if you believe you've already had that Dream Life, only to have in unfairly or unexpectedly taken from you, I am here to show you how to dream a New Dream, go after it and obtain it with a certainty that you deserve it.

CHAPTER ONE

TRANSFORMING IMPERFECTION INTO ACCEPTANCE

WHETHER the people you encounter in life are direct enough to say it to your face, or not, you can tell what they're thinking just by the way they look at you or interact with you. You know it all too well and you are frankly fed up with it: the looks of pity from relatives at holiday gatherings because of your divorce, the cute guy at the bar looking right past you to your model-cute bestie because you are not his "type", former work friends no longer inviting you out because you've been let go from your job, being cast out of your tight-knit Mommy group because you don't agree with one of their views on parenting. The judgmental comments about WHATEVER makes you different or imperfect in the eyes of another have completely affected how you feel about yourself. For me, it's the uncomfortable stares at the middle and ring fingers partially missing from my left hand and the obvious pointing at the jagged Z-plasty scars encircling my lower right leg that elicit rude whispers from strangers when I wear shorts, skirts or dresses that happen to put my bare calves on display in public.

Here you are, just living your life when you are unexpectedly faced with a reminder that you are different and NOT in a good way. All too often, we are confronted with someone who just cannot pass up the opportunity to point out our failures, differences or shortcomings. At least most well-meaning folks will try to disguise their desire to shame or judge you as an attempt at offering a helpful bit of advice. These interactions often leave you feeling sad, angry or embarrassed and thinking to yourself, "Gee, thanks for the reminder, I magically forgot, but I clearly have to be brought down another notch or two to soothe your fragile ego, right?" It hurts enough to make you want to lock yourself in your room for a week and just CRY or engage in some other equally negative, self-defeating behavior. So you do, but it always ends the same way. You feel worse, defeated and powerless. Here's the good news, I know that you picked up this book because you are looking for more than fluffy answers and meaningless platitudes. You are ready for a change. You know that you are more than just a product of your current circumstances. You are ready to move forward.

My Thanksgiving Turkey

It was mid-November 1978, I was 4 years old and just like the rest of my classmates at Uleta Daycare in North Miami, I was excited about Thanksgiving. Even at such a young age, I knew that it meant a big family get-together, a joyful celebration and spending time in the family kitchen. All of the women in my family were happily buzzing around the kitchen and dining room chatting, sharing and preparing special holiday recipes that result in tables filled with delicious food. Meanwhile, the men watched football, grunted their occasional displeasure at the outcome of various plays onscreen and barked the occasional request for another beer.

Among the various Fall-themed craft activities our teachers had us doing, there was the "hand turkey" project. We excitedly gathered the materials to put together our handmade art, knowing that we would be bringing these creations home to the delight of our families. The "hand turkey" was created by placing our left hand on a clean sheet of orange construction paper, having our teacher help us neatly trace the outline of our hand with black permanent marker and then giving us the task of coloring in our "hand turkey"; decorating it with our choice of autumn-hued feathers and beads. I waited patiently for my teacher, Ms. Smith, to make her way around the classroom. She efficiently traced one student's hand after another, making the odd pit stop to keep one or morenof us from eating paste or spilling too many beads. The anticipation built as I watched her walk down row after row of students, gradually making her way closer to me. She finally hovered over my tiny frame, looking down at my little left hand eagerly placed on the sheet, ready to become a work of art. Without explanation, she moved my left hand out of the way, replacing it with my right and traced it instead. Seeing the rest of the children around me busily coloring and decorating their turkeys with feathers, I naturally followed suit as Ms. Smith moved on to the next child. It wasn't until after our class returned from the lunch room that afternoon, seeing each of our projects hung up on the wall behind her desk, that EVERYONE noticed that all of the turkeys were facing the same direction except one, MINE. Amidst the ensuing whispers, looks, and pointing, Ms. Smith pulled me aside and bluntly explained that if she'd traced my left hand my turkey would not look "right" because some of the feathers would be too short, and that my right hand was "just perfect".

Looking back, I'm sure this was not an ill-intentioned act. It was probably the quickest, easiest way for her to deal with the situation front of her and continue doing her job. Perhaps she even may have felt she was doing me a favor. I will always remember this as the first moment that I felt different – because someone else told me I was. I have no real memory of the rest of that day. I do not remember crying or even feeling hurt. I am fairly certain that I did not even mention it when I came home that afternoon. As a young child, home was my safe space, my happy place. At home, I was just Maxine: daughter, sister, typical middle child. In that environment, I found love, happiness, structure, discipline, value, and understanding. With my immediate family, I was NOT the "disabled" child, nor was I considered less than my sisters.

REALITY CHECK: You Don't Have To Be Perfect To Be Worthy

Self-acceptance is the first key to transforming

your Imperfect life. Whether you had an encouraging voice in your life to plant those seeds in your heart and mind or not, there is a part of you that must be reminded now. It is time for you to know, not just pretend, that you have value. You may not feel worthy of acceptance......TOO BAD. It is time for you to put those feelings aside and get real. You cannot move your life forward into a positive, productive place without accepting yourself, period. (Oh, were you expecting some fluffy, cheerful "you can do it" – type sentiment? Yeah, I don't do that.....moving on!) If you'd like to stop and whine for a bit about how you can't find anything about yourself worthy of acceptance because "he", "she" or "they" never did, that's fine. Just put this book back down and I'll be right here once you've finished the pity party and are ready to get to work. Don't worry, I'll wait.

Now, that may seem a bit harsh, but it is time for you to understand that self-pity and blame are just going to get in the way of your progress. Sure, there will be moments in life that will tear you down. Certainly, you will have moments where you are overcome with negative emotions and fall apart, everyone does, we're all human. Your mission from now on is to let those "moments" be just that – "moments", not "derailments" that completely take you off-track into the abyss.

Let's get to work. I'm not going to bore you with some trite comparison of your life to some "glass half full" scenario. You are not a glass. Your life is not some plain, boring, non-descript glass devoid of anything to offer the world. Your life is an exquisite, hand-etched, Tiffany & Co. crystal champagne flute that sparkles in the sun, beaming back prisms of light and magnetically attracting the finest French champagne to fill it to overflowing. Take a moment to fully realize what that means. Think about the places such a fine champagne flute goes, the shelf it sits on, the dining room it is accustomed to, the care with which the champagne flute is handled, the status and stature of the person who sips from it. You may see yourself now as that half-empty glass, barely deserving of a thing. That ends now. You must be willing to accept yourself, imperfections and all. You must know with complete certainty that the very fact that you are alive, breathing and reading these words serves as proof that you are worthy of acceptance and that acceptance begins with you.

READY SET GO

Ready

What is the biggest Imperfection in my life?

_____

_____

_____

How has this Imperfection negatively impacted my life?

_____

_____

_____

Set

What words have I said to myself or behaviors have I displayed to reinforce my negative belief around my circumstance?

_____

_____

_____

Go

What positive change do I desire to see in my life in regards to my circumstances?

_____

_____

_____

What Functional Phrases can I create to reprogram my mind around my issue?

_____

_____

_____

What positive behaviors can I begin to display to reinforce my new, positive belief in regards to my circumstances?

_____

_____

_____

CHAPTER TWO

TRANSFORMING YOUR ATTITUDE INTO GRATITUDE

"Gratitude can change your life." "Start each day with gratitude." "Make a list of everything you're grateful for each night before you go to bed." "Just be grateful!"

DID reading all of that annoy you as much as it just annoyed me to write it? Of course, it did. First comes the right mindset: accepting yourself, forgiving yourself, building up your self-worth and rejecting negative voices from your inner circle. Without this, you cannot be in an effective state of mind to truly practice or even feel gratitude. Trying to express gratitude in any meaningful way without being in your "right mind" is like cooking a beautiful, delicious, satisfying meal for dinner by preparing it in dirty pots and them eating it off of dirty dishes. Truthfully, gratitude actually matters, however, we are not usually taught how to apply it to our lives in a way that has an impact. Too often, we are told to "just be grateful". Whenever the "just" comes before gratitude, it literally negates it. "Just be grateful." Sounds slightly dismissive. "Just be grateful" sounds like "you're lucky it wasn't worse". "Just be grateful" sounds like some phony magic words that should instantly make your whole life better. "Just be grateful" sounds like you're glad my situation didn't happen to you and furthermore you have no intention of offering me any real help with mine.

Gratitude Starts At Home

I was born in South Florida, the middle child of 3 girls. My immigrant parents left their home in Jamaica with a desire to raise a family and live The American Dream. As if that was not a daunting enough challenge, I came along in 1974 and was born with an extremely rare birth disorder called Amniotic Band Syndrome. To spare you the gory details, I'll simply share the highlights of how ABS affected me. I was born without a fully formed ring finger or middle on my left hand/left foot and endured a surgery shortly after birth on my right ankle that resulted in a very visible 360-degree scar around my right ankle. There are a few other minor details regarding other scars and pain, but overall I have not let my physical differences deter me from living a life that I love and achieving many of my dreams. I found the love of my life over 20 years ago, married him and we have two beautiful daughters. As a certified Youth Fitness Instructor, I've built my dream business, STARcise, a program that inspires young children to lead active, healthy lives and teaches them that every child can be a S.T.A.R. – Smart, Talented, Athletic, Respected ™. My life so far continues to be a beautiful journey of ups and downs, thanks to the ability to accept my imperfections and overcome the obstacles along the way.

My parents decided that I was the same as my sisters, meaning I was expected to bring home the same good grades, do the same chores and behave as the same proper, polite young lady that my sisters were, this led to me being grateful for being complimented on my manners. When I struggled to carry a laundry basket by handles that were too thick for me to fully get my shorter fingers around, I was expected to figure it out. Whenever I attempted to hand my father a jar full of pickles or peanut butter because it was tough for me to grasp with only two fingers and a thumb, it was handed right back to me because he believed that I could open it myself. This led me to be grateful that I was able to figure out solutions for these physical challenges and grateful that I did not have to wait for anyone else to help me or do things for me. This gratitude eventually led to a level of self-confidence I have today that is unbreakable. You might think my parents were being tough on me, maybe even callous, unhelpful or unfair. The truth is, they were being <u>strong</u> for me and I am grateful that they knew how to lend me strength until I learned to be strong for myself.

For my young parents, the 70's were an era without sonograms or support groups to guide them through the challenges of raising me, a child with a disability outside of their scope of experience. They came from their home island of Jamaica to the United States with only each other. No parents, siblings, relatives or friends nearby to lean on. By the time I was born, they already had my sister Nancy, born five years earlier, to take care of. Undeterred, my mother and father forged ahead in the spirit of love to raise me. To ensure that I never doubted my place in our family, my father Maxwell named me after himself. To ensure that I never doubted the strength, ability or purpose of my left hand, my mother literally shadowed me throughout my toddler years to pull any crayon, pencil, marker, chalk or even a stick that found its way into my right hand away from there and placed it firmly in my left hand, effectively making me left-handed. I never knew the enormity of their decisions, nor did I see the strength in the choices they made on my behalf until decades later, but I know now that so much of my strength and self-image came from the seeds my parents planted in my childhood. The outside world may never look at me and see "normal" or "regular" and that is fine by me. Being raised in a family where I knew I was "accepted" made it possible for me to accept myself, which is the foundation for every bit of strength I've summoned from within me to face the hardships that come into my life. The daily life within the walls of my childhood home became the training ground where I learned to fend for myself, defend myself and depend on myself for a complex range of little challenges, all while being loved and valued as a member of the family. Of course, my parents would often give my sisters and I the usual reminders of what we ought to be grateful for, too. I absolutely remember being told that "Children in Africa are starving" in order to make sure we ate our vegetables and that "There are people sleeping on the streets every night", in order to ensure that we made our beds and kept our rooms clean. The inference always was that we should be grateful for the little luxuries in our lives because there was always someone who did not have what we did. As much as I'd disagree with them in my mind, I understood that I had plenty to be grateful for. As a middle child, I would try to fuss that my older sister, Nancy, had a later bedtime than me or that my younger sister, Sonya had more dolls or toys than me. My feeble attempts at gaining extra attention were typically met with "Be grateful that you have sisters". What I know now to be true all these years later, is just how right my parents were all along. My sisters are both strong women and amazing mothers in their own right and I am grateful to have them both in my life.

REALITY CHECK: Your Life Doesn't Have To Be Perfect For You To Be Grateful

If the concept of gratitude still seems foreign to you, let's make it very simple. Being grateful for your life makes your life more enjoyable. You can scale this up or down to whatever degree you choose and it will still hold true. From the seemingly inconsequential: simply being grateful for being able to open your eyes in the morning, to the definitely monumental: gratitude on your wedding day, big promotion, graduation, the birth of a child, etc. Having a grateful attitude makes life better and having a funky attitude makes it worse, period. The key to activating gratitude in your life is this: gratitude comes first. This is the moment to ignore the little voice in your head that is tempting you to be lazy and trying to convince you that you can wait to be grateful when your situation improves, or when you have something better to be grateful for. If you have heard the saying "whoever can be trusted with little, can also be trusted with much", then you have already been taught a key part of how gratitude works: being grateful for your life "as is" clears the way for you to receive bigger, better and more to be grateful for.

To further drive home the point that gratitude comes first is not some "pie in the sky" idea, but rather a concept that you are likely to be very accustomed to, let's eat. Yes, let's eat. Imagine that you are sitting around the table with your loved ones, the air is thick with the aromas of a beautiful Sunday dinner and then someone says Grace. That's right! Before you eat, you said "Thank You" to bless the food. It is a very common practice for people to say a quick prayer of thanks prior to eating a meal. Many families use the simple "God is great, God is good, let us thank him for our food" with their children. Another common one, "For the food which we are about to receive, let us be truly grateful." Different religions and cultures have their own versions but the one common theme throughout is that gratitude comes first. Make a habit of using these simple concepts that already feel familiar to you in order to train your brain to get used to being grateful before you receive and you will see and feel a real change in your life.

READY SET GO

Ready

How has a lack of gratitude negatively impacted my life?

_____

_____

_____

Set

What words have I said to myself or behaviors have I displayed to reinforce my feeling ungrateful about my circumstance?

_____

_____

_____

Go

What can I genuinely say I am grateful for in my life today?

_____

_____

_____

What Functional Phrases can I create to rebuild my mind around Gratitude and what I am actually grateful for in my life?

_____

_____

_____

What positive actions can I take to reinforce my Grateful Attitude?

_____

_____

_____

CHAPTER THREE

TRANSFORMING

BELIEF INTO

KNOWLEDGE

FAITH and belief are wonderful. Having faith that a certain situation will work itself out gives you the strength to endure a hardship. Believing in another person's ability to come through for you gives you the patience to endure the process of waiting for the moment when they do. But knowledge, knowledge gives you the power to move forward with COMPLETE CONFIDENCE. Knowledge gives you the kind of confidence that simply does not recognize anything except what your mind accepts as truth. This may surprise you, but knowledge creates your feelings. You can feel what you know inside yourself. We often refer to this as intuition, however, the knowledge you have about yourself is directly connected to how you are feeling about yourself. Knowledge creates your confidence: when you know you have studied all of the material for a particular test, you are confident that you can ace the test. When you know that you are beautiful, you feel beautiful, that beauty radiates from within and shows up in the physical world in your smile, your posture and in the way you literally light up a room when you enter it.

Almost A Model

As a teen, I was awkward, shy, very thin and an easy target for the bullies both in my school and in my neighborhood. I was regularly taunted for my skinny legs, deformed ankle, kinky hair, inability to speak up, complete lack of friends and naturally, the obvious lack of those10 fingers and toes that at least could have made me "normal". Walking home from school, teen boys would comment that I would be physically undesirable until I "grew a butt". The mean girls in the hallway with lockers next to mine ridiculed the idea that anyone would ever want to marry me because my left hand was missing an actual finger to put a decent ring on. I usually ignored the painful comments and shook them all off because I knew deep down that I was not the person that the other children portrayed me to be. Part of how I dealt with the usual teenage self-consciousness was to start hiding my flaws and physical imperfections by wearing closed-toe shoes that never exposed my lack of toes, wearing long pants and skirts to keep anyone from seeing my ankle and keeping my hand in my pockets to avoid giving anyone the opportunity to stare or sling insults my way. Unfortunately, despite my best efforts at concealment coupled with all of the confidence built into me by my upbringing, nothing on Earth could have kept me from crying right in the middle of Wood Shop class on the first day of seventh grade. Just after taking attendance, Mr. Johnson jumped right into his usual speech about how we all needed to be careful around the band saws and other dangerous equipment in the classroom, or else we could lose a finger. His speech was unexpectedly interrupted by the poorly stifled giggles that grew into uncontrollable laughter coming from the two boys seated in front of me. They both turned around, staring right at me, wildly waving their left hands in my face with their ring and middle fingers curled up to imitate mine, shouting "too late!" at me in unison. Mr. Johnson swiftly reprimanded them and continued to read us the rest of his classroom rules as the tears streamed down my cheeks. I bravely wiped those tears away and made it through the rest of my day. Walking home, I debated whether I should even bother to mention the incident to my Mother. She was likely to just brush it off with a comment about how I was just fine the way I was when I was just looking for a little sympathy to go with my pity party. I understand now that her "tough love" style of parenting was exactly what I needed in order to toughen up and steel myself against the nastiness I'd endure in the years that followed. Back in those days, though, I believed that she just lacked the compassion that I was looking for. It was rare to hear anything complimentary from her; so rare in fact, that I still remember the day when that finally changed.

Most of the girls I grew up with in North Miami loved going to the 163rd Street Mall. I remember it being the one place where everyone went with their friends after school and on the weekends to chat with boys, shop for the latest outfits and just hang out. The closest I'd ever got to the Mall was to stare at it from the back seat of the family Oldsmobile as were on our way to or from church. The main exceptions were for "Back To School" shopping or during the holidays to buy gifts and I always went with my mother. I didn't go with friends, which never really bothered me on account of not really having any. It was on one of these rare occasions that something amazing happened. Walking through the mall, my mother and I were approached by a neatly dressed, handsome man in a suit. He engaged my mother in small talk before getting right to his point – ME! He complimented me on my general appearance, kindly inquired as to whether she had ever considered signing me up for modeling classes before and confidently declared that I'd be a great potential candidate for his agency. He somehow convinced my Mother to bring me in for an appointment back at his office as he produced a glossy business card with his company information on it. I was shocked when she agreed but I kept my feelings to myself for fear that she'd change her mind if I appeared too excited. I felt myself walking a bit taller in the days that followed, even smiling more. Here was someone who was filling my head with compliments and interest, the very thing I had been craving to boost my waning ego. The following week, I found myself sitting next to my mother in his office, wearing my nicest church dress. His office was rather ordinary and small, but clean and well organized. The walls were covered with large black and white headshots and colorful comp cards displaying the beautiful faces of dozens of teen girls and a few handsome boys. I felt terribly out of place yet this gentleman sat across from us in a luxuriously stuffed leather chair and promised an experience that would increase my confidence: modeling classes, photo shoots and maybe some catalog work. As he pulled the pricing sheet onto his desk that detailed the cost for this once in a lifetime opportunity, he turned his attention intently on my mother, asking if she thought I had what it took to benefit from such a program. For the very first time in my life, I heard my mother say these words, "Yes. I know that my daughter is beautiful and I believe that she can do anything that she sets her mind to." I remember looking at her and briefly wondering "Who was this woman?", but I felt such validation from her words that I never saw her the same way again. At this point he gestured for me to stand up and walk to the back of the room and then back towards his desk so that he could critique my walk. I slowly rose to my feet, determined to channel my best model walk and stepped as ladylike as I could to the back of the room, then back to my seat. I sat there, proudly awaiting his next words. When my eyes met his, I was not expecting for his face to look so visibly uncomfortable. I couldn't help but also notice that the pricing sheet was now conspicuously missing from view. A few moments of silence passed before he mumbled something about me being almost pretty enough to be a model but that he just wouldn't know how to hide my fingers and or my leg from the photos. He apologized for wasting our time and claimed he should have noticed it when he first saw me that day in the Mall. As he hastily ushered us out of his place of business, my mother didn't say a word. We just got in the car and drove home. I don't remember being terribly disappointed about the experience, because she didn't make too big a deal of it. What I do remember and what stays with me to this very day were her kind words of belief in me and her verbal confirmation of confidence in me. It wasn't until years later that I began to develop my own "self talk" routine to increase my self confidence, but I know that hearing those words from her made it possible for me to know that I did indeed have what it takes to do whatever I set my mind to. While, I never ended up working as a model. I did have the confidence in myself to audition for the *Wheel Of Fortune* game show several years later and I actually got cast to be a contestant on the show. It was a whirlwind experience and so much fun meeting Pat Sajak and Vanna White. I am proud to say that the casting agents chose me because I was great at playing the game, I brought unique personality and natural energy to the show. Not only was I chosen *regardless* of my physical differences, no one asked me to hide my hand when I finally made it on to the set to film the show with the my fellow contestants. After the episode aired, I was even contacted by the producers of *Wheel Of Fortune* to write a blog post about my experiences on filming the show for the Wheel Of Fortune Website.

REALITY CHECK: Knowledge Is Power

Imagine yourself coming home at the end of the day. See yourself pull into the driveway, get out of your car, lock the car door, walk through the front door of your home, lock that door behind you and flip on the light switch by the front door as you step inside. Now, ask yourself: Did any of those activities require ACTIVE faith or belief or your part? No! You pulled into the driveway because you KNOW how to drive and you KNOW that your car will stop when you put it into park. You walked to your front door because you KNOW that your legs and feet are able to carry you that distance and you KNOW how to walk. You flipped the light switch because you KNOW that the electricity works and you KNOW that the light bulb will illuminate the room. You easily just visualized yourself doing something you had done hundreds or thousands of times because your mind just knew what to do. Your imagination automatically placed you into a familiar routine, there was no conscious thought required. As you imagined yourself coming home just now, were you worried that your legs would buckle underneath you as you walked? Did you fear that the car would not stop when you stepped on the brakes and put the car in park? Were you praying that the lights would come on when you flipped the light switch? Of course not, you moved forward in complete confidence because of the knowledge you have. This is the kind of knowledge you must have in order to activate your new beliefs about yourself and your life so that your brain takes in this new information and accepts it without effort. Your goal is to build your self-confidence with the KNOWLEDGE that you are worthy, you are loved and your imperfections do not define you. There is no point in just blindly repeating some weak "feel good" phrases because your brain KNOWS better and will reject your attempt to trick your mind into feeling better. Doing so will just leave you in the same place or worse, feeling as though something you tried simply did not work.

As a child, most of your knowledge and confidence came from your everyday experiences: you learned about yourself and the world around you by the information you took in through your five senses. You learned about gravity when you fell down or threw toys and saw them fall to the ground instead of floating up into the atmosphere. You learned about hot and cold by eating food, taking baths and feeling the temperature around you. You learned what baby food you liked by tasting it. You learned the sound of your mother's voice as she sang you to sleep each night. You learned the smell of your father's cologne as he carried you back to our crib. As you grew up, your knowledge and confidence grew and was built in a deeper way by what you were told by other people: this includes lessons learned in school through class assignments and homework. You learned your last name, the various members of your family and certain family traditions and beliefs by what your parents and relatives told you, as well as what they told you to do. Most importantly, you learned what you currently believe about yourself and your abilities mostly through what other people told you as well. You may have had supportive parents growing up, an encouraging teacher that took an interest in you along the way or just your friends or even strangers commenting on your appearance at certain points in your life. Every positive or negative word that was spoken to you has had an impact on how you think and feel about YOU. It is now up to you to put yourself in the driver's seat and take control of what your brain KNOWS. Give yourself permission, love yourself and decide that you can accept the knowledge that is required to build these new beliefs. It is time for you to be able to say "I know " with genuine confidence and truly know that you are worthy, you are loved and your imperfections do not define you, nor can they defeat you. By this point, you already know that this book is not here to serve you some cheery, false "motivation". You already know what you have inside of you, so let's jump into the tools that will help you take the next step.

READY SET GO

Ready

What is my biggest negative belief I have about myself?

_____

_____

_____

Set

What words have I said to myself or behaviors have I displayed to reinforce my negative belief about myself?

_____

_____

_____

Go

What positive beliefs must I KNOW about myself?

_____

_____

_____

What Functional Phrases can I create to reprogram my mind from belief to knowledge?

_____

_____

_____

What positive behaviors can I begin to display to reinforce my new knowledge about myself?

_____

_____

_____

CHAPTER FOUR

TRANSFORMING OUTER VOICES INTO INNER STRENGTHS

NOW, let's take a moment to address the voices outside of your head that are calling you unworthy. Similar to how the voices in your head have been holding you back, the actual voices of the people in your life can have an equally, if not greater, damaging effect. This is why accepting and forgiving yourself first is critical. It does not matter who it is: parent, teacher, spouse, relative, boss, co-worker, friend, ex, nosy neighbor, child, etc. Even if the person in your life is well-meaning in their intent, having your actions questioned and challenged will drag you down and hold you there if you let it.

Just A Trip To The Nail Salon

High school graduation was only a few weeks away and some of the girls from our Senior class were discussing getting their nails done for the ceremony. Call it nerves, fear or insecurity, but I never made it to the salon in time to have cute French tips before I crossed the stage and collected my diploma. It happened about a month later, when I chose not to think about it and just go for it. There was only one nail shop I knew of, Pretty Nails, right across the street from the 163rd Street Mall. I walked into the little salon and there sat a lovely Korean man, his wife and eldest daughter sitting at their stations doing manicures. I signed my name on the little sign-up sheet on the little reception desk before me, sat in an available seat alongside the other customers and waited to hear my name called. As I leafed through the well-worn fashion magazines and nail shop catalogs, I realized that there were more colors and styles that were trending than just a simple French manicure. I marveled at the wall of polish colors in the little shop and noticed a display with sample nails designs: gems and glitter and artwork, oh my! My young mind raced with the possibilities. Before long, the youngest nail tech innocently mispronounced my name and motioned me over to her station, set between two older ladies enjoying their own nail experience. Their enjoyment came to an end, however, once I sat down. Upon glancing over at my short, colorless nail beds, it was apparent that I had only 8 fully formed fingers. The disgust and eventual anger that this caused in the lady on my left boiled over into loudly commenting that it was not only unfortunate for me, but also very, very wrong of me to force the poor cosmetician to have to touch those gross things. The fact that I did not have the decency to stay at home and figure out how to polish my own nails was the topic of conversation between her and the lady to my right who passionately agreed. The two of them made it their mission to berate, condemn and insult me into hopefully going away. The odd appearance of my hands had caused such fear and discomfort in these two, that I endured their nasty stares, disapproving grunts, impatient sighs and an endless barrage of rude questions for the next several minutes: What's wrong with her? Why would she even come in here with that? Who does she think she is? All the while, I did my best to ignore them, engage my kind nail lady in conversation and try to inwardly and outwardly enjoy my very first set of acrylic nails. Fortunately, these ladies were done with their own manicures and headed out to leave well before me. As they trudged off towards the exit, bothered by their inability to rid themselves of my existence, they could only mutter a few parting shots about it all being "just a shame". To this day, I wrote them off as products of an era that was taught to hide imperfections rather than acknowledge them. That night, however, I pulled together all of the love, self-confidence and courage that I had been instilled with at the tender age of 18 and refused to allow small minds to influence me. I would love to tell you that I walked out of that place with my head held high and adored my new beautiful nails all the way home. Actually I did, but between my triumphant exit and the ride home, I sat in my car for several minutes and just cried. Sure, I was bullied in school and had endured the stares before, but the pain I felt was about more than just these two mean older women. My tears came with the realization that my childhood was not going to be the end of it. I sat there knowing that I would deal with ignorance for the rest of my life and that I would have to continue to be stronger and stronger. I was overcome with the sheer exhaustion of knowing that I had my whole life ahead of me: dreams, goals, plans, hopes and that whatever I achieved would be fought for at a permanent disadvantage . Once the tears dried, I looked at how cute my nails were and resolved in that moment to always get my nails done whenever I wanted them done, in whatever color or style I chose, because regardless of how anyone else felt, I enjoyed how they made me feel. Looking back, If there was one thing I could go back and tell my teenage self sitting in tears behind wheel, I would have told myself that getting my nails would actually lead to some pretty great moments in my future. It turns out that getting my nails done in wild colors, different lengths and sparkly designs has become part of my signature style. I am so well known for getting all 8 of my nails done in a glittery and colorful way that everyone notices that I actually ended up being cast as a client on a fun reality show that was being filmed at a local nail salon call *Boss Nails,* which aired on the Oxygen Network. The show followed the adventures of an exceptional nail artist named Dana Cody and her talented staff whose personalities are just as wild as the manicures they produce. The day I came into the salon, I ended up with 8 perfect canvases of blue and yellow glitter, gems and gorgeousness!!! One of my nails even looked a bit like the logo on my business card. The night it aired was bittersweet for me, my family and friends were watching all across the country so I was keeping up with the comments on social media. Unfortunately, I did see a few comments from complete strangers on Twitter that brought me right back to that first manicure in North Miami. The hateful comments were flying about how I only had 8 fingers and should be embarrassed that I had the nerve to ask for a discount. I didn't let that ruin my fun, however, I decided that the good outweighed the bad and made sure to record the episode for my own enjoyment.

REALITY CHECK: You Can Be Great

I am not going to coddle you with some goofy statement about how nasty comments say more about the person speaking them to you than it does about you. That is just simple, common sense and maddeningly unhelpful. It's akin to a young boxer standing in the practice ring as punches from his opponent coming flying in his direction. Would it be practical for his trainer to just yell from outside the ring that his sparring partner is just "being a jerk" for punching him the head, or would that boxer be better served if he were armed with tactical moves to succeed in the ring? Knowing that you are worthy of the change you desire in your life is the armor that you must cover yourself with in order to survive the onslaught of stupidity that comes out of someone else's mouth, regardless of their intention.

Take a moment to make a mental checklist of the people in your life. See those people in your inner circle insulting, blaming and judging you for being broken over your current situation? They will be the first ones lining up to crush you even harder when they notice that you are finally stepping out of the fog of sadness, holding your head up a bit more and taking the action to move forward and create a change that improves your life. Why? Because your negative situation was providing a distraction from some imperfection in their own lives. I have never encountered a person in my life who pointed out my imperfections that didn't have insecurities of their own! You are not required to take on this burden. Proximity may make it impossible to avoid having to hear it, but it is completely within your power to keep it from entering your mind and affecting your thoughts or actions, period.

READY SET GO

Ready

Who are the people in my inner circle that are the most critical of my situation?

_____

_____

_____

How have their voice/comments negatively impacted

my life?

_____

_____

_____

How have I allowed their actions negatively impacted
my life?

_____

_____

Set

What words have I said to myself or behaviors have I
displayed to reinforce their negative words about my
situation?

_____

_____

_____

Go

What positive change do I desire to see in my reaction
to their negative words?

_____

_____

_____

What Functional phrases can I create to block, disable
and replace the negative words of others?

_____

_____

_____

What positive behaviors can I begin to display to protect myself from those harmful, unhelpful words?

_____

_____

CHAPTER FIVE

TRANSFORMING NEGATIVE EMOTION INTO FORWARD FOCUS

THERE is a difference between being sensitive and being emotional. Sensitivity speaks more to your ability to truly feel various emotions and to sympathize with the emotions of others. Being emotional really speaks to a lack control, giving in to the emotion beyond the point of reason. Being emotional usually carries consequences when the emotion is negative rather than positive. Imagine yourself in the presence of someone that is crying, arguing, fighting, complaining or insulting and cannot seem to stop themselves. You can probably think back to a moment or two where even you have indulged in a bit of emotional behavior. You may have even felt justified in it. But, what did you accomplish in that moment? Negative emotions never yield positive results! Mind you, I am NOT suggesting that you train your mind to become a Stepford clone that never cries or feels any type of negative emotion, that is neither reasonable nor emotionally healthy. Truthfully, anyone can be an emotional wreck, just allowing the circumstances of life to carry them uncontrollably from one extreme to another and reacting to the environment around them. You can choose to be in a constant state of balance – only dipping into the lower, negative emotional state for brief periods, yet easily capable of reaching and enjoying higher, positive emotional states such as joy, happiness, and peace.

Daddy's Girl

Being the middle child comes with its own set of circumstances. For every scientific study that claims middle-born children grow up one way, you can certainly find a psychologist somewhere that will claim the opposite. For me, I took being the middle child quite literally. When our family traveled together, there I was in the backseat of the car, sitting in the middle, between my two sisters. When we ate as a family, I sat between my two sisters. If we sat on the sofa to watch television in the family room, I took the spot right in the center. Whenever we had to take turns playing, I always went next, right after my big sister. In pretty much every situation growing up, I was in the middle of my two sisters: my eldest who got to do everything first and my youngest who was the baby of the family. My sisters and I had our fair share of squabbles and arguments as other typical siblings and we loved each other just much. As the middle child, I always found myself in the middle of doing something that required attention and the one person I required the most attention from was my father. Being his namesake produced two distinctly different outcomes: on the one hand, I grew up with a strong sense of belonging to our family because I carried the name of our patriarch. On the other hand, I sought his approval with every little thing I did. My father was not overly emotional or hands-on, he was home very rarely due to his intense work schedule. When he was home, he preferred to relax with the newspaper or watching sports, choosing to isolate himself rather than engage and interact with the family. We did have "family moments" though. He was always with us at church, he occasionally took the family out for a dinner or breakfast at the Denny's nearby our home and he definitely made a point of taking us to football games during the season. I even remember the Summer of 1986 where we went on an extended family vacation and spent a great deal of quality time together. His general parenting style leaned more toward pushing us to do better than whatever our effort produced. Once he taught me to swim, he expected me to learn how to swim faster. After successfully learning to write with the few fingers I had on my left hand, he expected me to learn to write in cursive. When I got a 98% A on my report card, he expected me to bring home a 100% A+. Time and again, I rose to the occasion, achieving the various goals set before me, never receiving praise from him, but steadily growing in confidence in myself. My ability to succeed at the tasks he constantly set before me, led me to believe that these achievements made me valuable to him.

My senior year became my own personal "Trifecta Of Achievement": I graduated near the top of my class, I got accepted into my college of choice and my grades got myself a full scholarship to cover my tuition. Although my whole family was in attendance at my graduation, including several relatives, as I walked across the stage in a cap and gown to receive my diploma the only person I looked for in the crowd of familiar faces belonged to my father. Once the ceremony ended, I headed straight for him to offer that shiny sheet of paper with my name on it as another token of my worth. Regardless of the flood of cards, hugs, words of praise and pats on the back that came from the rest of my family, friends, and relatives that night, I stayed by my father's side and hung on his every word of pride and encouragement. The days that followed were a blur of joy and excitement, I faced the adjustment of leaving high school and preparing to attend college in the Fall. I had every expectation of being given a new set of goals to achieve in order to receive further validation from my father in this new journey. So, it came as a complete shock when he suddenly packed up and left the country, abandoning my mother, my sisters and myself, with no explanation. My entire world had imploded on itself in an instant. He left our home on a Sunday morning, I watched him drive away and when the realization hit me that he was never coming back, I was completely lost. I ran to my bedroom, slammed the door and flung myself onto my bed, crying and screaming into my pillow until my throat sore. I spent the rest of my day in my room, unable to eat or speak. Every dream I had of my new future had been ripped out of me and I collapsed into a corner and determined that my whole life was over. Gone was any ambition to attend college or create a life of meaning or value. My mind teetered on the edge of insanity as I began to visualize ways to end my own life.

As the sun began to set, my mother came into my room and attempted to communicate with me. She saw that I was an unresponsive wreck and I had not eaten. In my mind at that moment, nothing anyone could say would have made an impact. Yet, in her kindness and wisdom, my mother pulled me up onto my feet, wiped my face, walked me to the kitchen, sat me at the table and began speaking to me in a series of "You Are" statements. As she placed a meal before me and sat down beside she said, "you are going to eat this dinner because I didn't cook for it to go to waste", "you are going to take a shower and get ready for bed", "in the morning, you are going to show me the Freshman Packet that came from the college so that we can get you prepared for school" and so on. My mother knew that there was nothing that she could say that would bring my father back, there was nothing that she could have told me that would change how hurt I was. She did know how to change my focus. By repeatedly telling me what I was going to do to, she was able to make me believe it. Without lowering herself to my depressed emotional state, she pulled me out of my fear, anger and sadness. By the steadiness, repetition, and conviction of her words, I was able to focus, gain a bit of my own strength, push through the Summer without my father, and get myself together, ready for my next adventure in college.

REALITY CHECK: I Don't Repeat Mantras, I Repeat Functional Phrases

You can use a variety of Functional Phrases and "I Am" statements to get you out of a space of "extreme emotions": God is too good, life is too good and I am too blessed. You can preface this with: "I am not going to give in to (anger, sadness, pity, shame, fear, etc) because God is too good, life is too good and I am too blessed. However, I do find myself just repeating the main phrase in rapid succession to pull myself back from a negative place when I feel those emotions running hot. You may not feel the truth in those words initially, but I challenge you to push through and continue until either the words feel true or your emotional state returns to a positive space. You will often find that a combination of both takes place as you repeat this practice. The key to getting immediate results from these phrases is to make them a part of your regular routine before you find yourself in need, this way you are able to "trigger" your brain into making the emotional shift more easily and genuinely.

READY SET GO

Ready

What is the biggest emotional trigger in my life?

_____

_____

_____

What negative emotion do I most easily revert to?

_____

_____

_____

Set

What words have I said to myself or behaviors have I displayed to reinforce my negative emotion?

_____

_____

_____

Go

What positive change do I desire to see in my life in regards to my emotions?

_____

_____

_____

What Functional phrases can I create to reprogram my mind to remain emotionally stable?

_____

_____

_____

What behaviors can I begin to display to reinforce my new, belief in positive emotions?

_____

_____

_____

CHAPTER SIX

TRANSFORMING

FAULT INTO

FORGIVENESS

AT the core of being able to genuinely accept yourself is forgiveness. You know that little nagging voice in the back of your mind that pops up to tell you that everything is your fault? The voice inside that says, "You created the circumstances, you chose that job you lost, the man who left, the car that broke down"? That voice is only partially right, so please understand what this voice is really telling you. What you hear is "Your situation is your fault, therefore you are unworthy of forgiveness. You screwed up your life so badly that it is irreversible. Wallow in this depression and don't you dare move on, ever." If this is what you've been hearing, honey, your translator is broken! The reason you keep hearing the voice in your head repeatedly is that you've not been able to address it. In the past, you've not faced the situation head-on, out of either fear, shame, guilt, sadness or just feelings of pain, overwhelm and denial. The great news is that you have the opportunity now to learn a lesson from your situation, gain knowledge and strength, then transform your situation and move forward.

At Least He Loves Me, I Think

Before I met my husband, I had a typical teenage case of puppy love that disguised itself as "true love wrapped in a toxic relationship". We met the night of my high school graduation and hit it off right away. We exchanged numbers and began our courtship over the phone. Hour-long conversations became the daily routine. He'd tell me how pretty I was, how cute my voice was, how he enjoyed talking to me and listening to me, too. I dove head-first into the romance of it all. Eventually, we began seeing each other, he regularly would come to my parents home just so we could sit together and talk face to face. The courtship slowly progressed to dates at the park, dinners and an occasional movie. At first, everything was perfect. Sort of. I was so excited to find someone who liked me that, like many women, I overlooked most of his faults and just focused on the positives until there weren't any left. I enjoyed the way he held doors and chairs for me in public, so I overlooked how he gradually became demanding in private. It felt so good to hold hands with him and be acknowledged as "his girl" in public that I overlooked how he would comment about the attractiveness of other women in front of me in private. I felt so grown and so mature for finally having a boyfriend in general, that I overlooked his immature and selfish behaviors that kept popping up. I loved being one of the few girls at my job who even had a boyfriend. I loved it so much that I overlooked how inappropriate it was for him to constantly give rides home to these other girls without me. Soon, I went from overlooking his faults to hiding the damage he was doing from others. Not because I wanted to protect him, but my ego was so wrapped in how much it could look and feel like I had the perfect relationship, that I lied out of a desire to just maintain the image. Finally, I had come to the point where his infidelity and abuse collided with my ego and emotions in such a way that I was forced to admit that I was in a toxic relationship and that it was time to end it. It didn't happen overnight, though. I suffered in a loveless and abusive relationship for several months before I had the strength to end it for real. It was like a strange tango: I would threaten, he would apologize, I would take him back and he would be sweet for a few days, then he would shove me and

I would retreat, he would pretend it was my fault and claim no one else would want me, fear of ending up alone brought me back to him and for a little while we would pretend to be okay with each other before it all went sideways again. When I finally got the courage up to get him out of my life, I was relieved that it was over but that relief soon turned into embarrassment over the situation I had found myself in. I faced the inevitable questions, insults and shaming from friends and family over my so-called perfect boyfriend. I took most of these questions to heart and began blaming myself for dating him in the first place. I tortured myself for staying with him, accepting his insults, being made a fool of and degraded by the man that supposedly loved me. For a very long time, in my mind, the problem was me. Somehow I deserved to be treated badly. Months went by as I agonized over every detail of my time with him. It got to a point where I nearly concluded that if I ever did find anyone else to love me, I would only be worthy of the same toxic relationship.

Fortunately, my young heart's desire was for my next relationship to be better than that train wreck. This desire led me to work on myself. In doing so, I found that the first step I had to take was to forgive myself.

I had done enough replaying of the old relationship in my mind that I knew what I had done wrong. It was time to get past the hurt and acknowledge that it was me who accepted his misbehavior time after time, it was me who hid his abuses from my inner circle and it was me who stayed way too long. I wrote letters and little notes to myself both apologizing to and forgiving myself for everything. I wrote promises to be the girl who deserved better and to find the right man for me. It didn't happen overnight, but eventually, I was able to face myself in the mirror and see a woman worthy of love. In reality, I had always been worthy, I just needed to forgive myself in order to move forward. Shortly thereafter, I did find love with the man who is now my husband. The woman he met back then was just as confident and just as loving as I am today. We are still together and continuing to build our life together well over 20 years later.

REALITY CHECK: It Starts With
Forgiveness

At this point, you may be wondering what you have to forgive yourself for in your current situation because you didn't cause it. I can almost hear you now, "But Maxine, my situation is like your Amniotic Band Syndrome. How can you forgive yourself for something you did not cause?" Here's the answer, look for your part in any of it, even the aftermath. Regarding my ABS, I have had to forgive myself multiple times throughout my life: for the times I let insecurity about my leg hold me back, for the moments I was angry or depressed about my fingers, about the split-second decisions I made to shamefully hide my scars in pictures in an effort to keep myself and others from seeing them. You know the truth about how you have judged, blamed, criticized or even mistreated yourself over your imperfections. It is time to take responsibility. Acknowledge it, own it – but then you must forgive yourself in order to move on. Don't you go to God to ask for forgiveness when you do wrong? Don't you go in prayer, confessing and owning up to your imperfections, then asking for (and receiving) that beautiful forgiveness? Don't we even go to our fellow man to ask for forgiveness when we've done them wrong? Yes? It is time to really get honest with yourself and genuinely forgive yourself. You must do whatever it takes: lock yourself in a closet, your car, a quiet room, write it down, speak it out, say it in the mirror. Own up, admit, confess, tell the truth, get very clear on exactly what you feel is your fault in your situation and then FORGIVE YOURSELF. Speak your whole name out loud and say, "I forgive you." Write it out as many times as you can until you fill a whole page, reading it out loud as you go. Stand in a mirror until the tears are streaming down your face and you finally believe that are forgiven. Forgive yourself for the big and the small. And then don't stop. Make it a point to end every night forgiving and asking forgiveness before you fall asleep. You will wake up new each morning and stronger than the day before. Truly practice the art of "forgive and forget". The next time you fall into the old habit of blaming yourself for the past, snap yourself out of it immediately

READY SET GO

Ready

What do I need to forgive myself for?

_____

_____

_____

How has blaming myself held me captive in my life?

_____

_____

_____

Set

What words have I said to myself or behaviors have I displayed to truly begin to forgive myself?

_____

_____

_____

Go

What positive change will I see in my life once I forgive myself?

_____

_____

_____

What Functional Phrases can I create to set my mind to know that I am forgiven for my past?

_____

_____

_____

What positive behaviors can I begin to display to reinforce my new, positive belief that I am Imperfect, but I am forgiven?

CHAPTER SEVEN

TRANSFORMING FEAR INTO A BETTER FUTURE

"YOU will not feel afraid anymore if you just start singing." This was the advice that a tiny, courageous koala gave to Meena: a shy elephant with a big, beautiful voice at the end of the animated hit movie *Sing*. Meena knew she wanted to sing and she knew her voice was worth hearing, but fear held her back to the point of literal paralysis. What happened next was nothing short of an "Imperfect" Hollywood ending. Armed with just enough courage to put one foot in front of the other, Meena headed out onstage towards the microphone awaiting her before the crowd. As she reached out for the mike stand, it tumbled over, striking a number of people on the front row. She stumbled, she stuttered, she stopped herself, but soon the silence was broken by her soft, sweet voice, capturing the hearts of everyone in the theater, including her critics. As she finally began singing, she got so caught up in the moment that as she hit and held a particularly spectacular high note, she caused the entire backdrop at the rear of the stage to completely crumble into a pile of rubble. Finally feeling fearless, she shrugged it off and finished her stellar performance. By just singing one song, a shy elephant with big dreams overcame her insecurities and transformed her present situation into a future headed in the direction of her dreams.

The Four Words That Changed My Life

It was just another weekday, I was a few years into a pretty serious relationship with my boyfriend, Joe. We lived together and we worked together in the same office. That evening, we were in the middle of our regular post-work routine: jogging about a mile or so down the beach and then walking back towards our little apartment, discussing work projects and weekend plans. I was so into the conversation that I never noticed that we had passed our place and were walking onto the beach towards a jungle gym on the sand. As we chatted surrounded by swings and slides under the stars, the conversation turned to the future. Joe sweetly began speaking of his love for me and his plans for a future that had me at the center of it. Staring intently into my eyes and holding out a golden circle of trust, he surprised me with the question that I had been longing to hear, "Will you marry me?"

Time froze in that moment, or more accurately, I froze. Joe and I had been dating each other for a few years at this point and I was certain of my love for him so the word "yes" should have come rushing out, but the fear of what I would be agreeing to flashed in my mind: marrying into a family that I already knew wasn't exactly thrilled with me. Through our few years of forced interactions and uncomfortable smiles, it was clear to me that I represented imperfection in their little perfect world. My brown skin, incomplete college education, and 8 fingers stood in glaring opposition to the Ivy league, Jewish, politician, socialite family that he came from. I had already faced the cold stares and impolite questions from the onset, yet managed to make it clear over time that I was not going anywhere because we loved each other. Taking on his last name, however, presented a different challenge: Was I ready to have his children, raise them, share a life with him and his family? Did I have what it took to make my own place in the world as his wife? Could I be Mrs. Haber and still maintain a sense of myself? Was I willing to overlook the possibility of awkward moments when he'd introduce me as his wife to new acquaintances in the future?

Once this life-altering question left his lips, the avalanche of my own questions hit my brain in rapid succession to the point of near dizziness. A gust of wind rushed between us as I focused on the expectant look on his face. Staring back at me I saw a look of hope, love, and confidence in his eyes that gave me all the courage I needed on that beautiful Autumn night in 1998 to smile back at him and finally say, "Yes!" Seemingly without a thought, Joe reached for my right hand to fit the ring onto the only ring finger I had. This simple innocent gesture spoke volumes to me in that moment. I knew that his love for me had nothing to do with my exterior and that he truly loved and accepted of ALL of me, not just the "perfect" parts. It also showed me a level of understanding that was rare for me to find outside of my family. My left ring finger cannot hold a ring on it, so he simply placed the ring on the next best thing. Also, knowing that I am "left-hand dominant", he finally gave my right hand something to be good for!

In the years that followed, I am proud to share that our lives have been a beautiful mess of the same highs and lows as most marriages: babies, houses, jobs, groceries, laundry, anniversaries, birthdays, etc. We have arguments and overreactions just like most couples. Our home is filled with pictures, proud moments and occasionally "peace and quiet". Through the good, the bad and the inconsequential we are still together and still enjoying the ride towards the future. It is not perfect, nor is it a disaster, rather, our love just IS. One truth that stands out is that none of what we have would be possible without his courage to ask, my courage to answer and our commitment to go forward together.

REALITY CHECK: What Is Fear Holding You Back From?

Let's focus on what your future looks like today. This is not the time to fantasize about "where you see yourself in five years". It is time to get real and face what your life looks like now based on your current decisions and what your life could look like when you make new decisions that can alter your current course and take you into the future you actually desire. First, understand that you arrived at your current situation as a result of your behavior, decisions, and mindset in your past. You could not have gotten here otherwise. You must be honest with yourself about what you have been afraid to choose and why. Take stock of where you are and understand that the areas you are dissatisfied with, you can change.

Change can take many forms: you can make a choice that changes where you live, work or play. I accomplished this when I moved my entire family to Nevada after living in Florida for over 40 years. You can change how you interact with people in your life or choose to remove them altogether. It took a firm decision, on my part, to love myself so much that I couldn't allow people into my inner circle that negatively impacted me and a choice to reject any negative words or actions from anyone in my circle that were unavoidable. Then there are the changes to how you choose to perceive the situations you cannot change. These are the tough ones, so you must face them first. I cannot change the fact that I was born with and will always live with my various physical differences. All the praying, wishing and positive thinking in the world cannot bring my fingers and toes back, nor will it magically correct my right ankle or right foot. I do have the power, though, to see myself as whole just as I am, to reject the notion that

I am inadequate, insufficient or disabled. I love myself as I am instead of hating myself for what I cannot change. The choice is simple, the change is not. Remember that knowledge alone is not power, applied knowledge is true power. A cookbook may contain a recipe you love so much that you've memorized it, but it's meaningless until you get into the kitchen and actually bake that cake!

READY SET GO

Ready

What am I most afraid of changing?

_____

_____

_____

What area of my life needs to change in order for me to move forward?

_____

_____

_____

Set

What negative words have I said or behaviors have I displayed that keep me from a better future for myself?

_____

_____

_____

Go

What positive change will I see in my life once I let go of the fear?

_____

_____

_____

What Functional phrases can I create to set my mind to release the fear and move into my desired future?

_____

_____

_____

What positive behaviors can I begin to display to reinforce my new, positive belief that I am fearless and deserving of a better future?

_____

_____

_____

MAXINE HABER

CHAPTER EIGHT

TRANSFORMING YOUR REAL LIFE INTO REAL LOVE

LOVE is commonly referred to as an emotion or a feeling. This is an elementary and slightly incomplete definition to explain such a complicated and multi-faceted energy. Yes, love is something you DO and something you can feel, but love is also the highest form of vibrational energy on Earth. Love begins at the source of all life, love is also a mindset that can literally keep you from being negatively impacted or emotionally devastated by outside influences. You can literally choose to create love and feel the love from inside yourself before anyone does anything to make you feel loved.

Unconditional Love

It was the moment that I had been waiting for ever since I received a positive pregnancy test. After nine months of growing inside of me, my firstborn child was just about to make her big debut. The moment had also been preceded by 14 hours and 19 minutes of labor in a birthing suite that included my pillows from home, my favorite Bob Marley CD playing in the background and an anxious husband at my side. All of the planning, preparation, and patience culminated in one final push as Jennifer made her entrance into the world and I made my way from young wife to young mother. I held in her my arms for the very first time as if she was a precious first place trophy I received upon crossing the finish line of a grueling triathlon. As I studied every detail of her tiny frame, an overwhelming and unfamiliar feeling of love for this beautiful child came over me. Love was not an unfamiliar concept to me: my family, husband, and friends loved me. But this was something new and special, it felt as if my heart was beating inside myself and in this little person at the same time.

REALITY CHECK: WHAT IS LOVE?

When I stated that love is something that you can choose to create and feel from inside yourself before anyone does anything to make you feel loved, I meant it. Let's do a quick little exercise to demonstrate my point. Think of your best friend surprising you at work with a grand bouquet of your absolute favorite flower. Imagine the lengths to which your friend went to plan the surprise, taking time off from their own job to bring you these flowers. Think of the sweet words of friendship and appreciation in the hand-written card that came with this gift. Imagine the sense of satisfaction your friend gets by seeing you thoroughly enjoy their presence and your overall surprise. Enjoy for a moment how all of this makes you feel. Now imagine you were handed flowers by a complete stranger. No note, not your favorite flower, no mention of your birthday. Do you even feel anything?

Imagine that these were given to you instead by someone who you consider an enemy. Have your feelings changed now? Maybe to anger, distrust, confusion? Understand that the physical flowers did not cause your happiness, neither did the person who gave it to you. The person with the flowers may have changed from one situation to the next but the feelings you felt were yours. You created those feelings inside yourself, you chose to feel whatever emotion you felt. Your mind placed a value on each individual based on your experience with them and that created your emotional outcome. When you are focused on going throughout your day tuned into the vibration of love energy, you will be able to enjoy and appreciate those flowers on their own, just for being flowers, regardless of who gave them to you.

READY SET GO

Ready

How have been showing myself hatred instead of love?

_____

_____

_____

How did I convince myself that I wasn't worthy of love?

_____

_____

_____

Set

What words have I said to myself or behaviors can I display to truly begin to feel that I am loved?

_____

_____

_____

Go

What positive change will I see in my life once I start truly loving myself?

_____

_____

_____

What Functional Phrases can I create to set my mind to know that I am loved?

_____

_____

_____

What positive behaviors can I begin to display to reinforce my new, positive belief that I am LOVED?

_____

_____

CHAPTER NINE

TRANSFORMING AFFIRMATIONS INTO ACTIONS

TRUE transformation does not happen overnight. It is going to take some real work on your part to get yourself to the place you desire to be in life. Just as you did not likely run immediately after taking your first step, you will not create lasting, positive change in your life by just reading a book or repeating some affirmations. You have within you the ability necessary to transform your troubles into triumphs, it is up to you take action. Much of what you have learned at this point in this book is simple, but "simple" is far cry from "easy". One of the key findings in the decades-long research study undertaken by Professor John Gottman was the "5:1 Rule". Gottman discovered that for every negative comment that enters your mind, it takes 5 positive ones to replace it in your mind (or the repetition of one positive comment a minimum of five times). This holds true whether you speak negatively to yourself, someone speaks a hurtful word to you or if you spew out an angry insult to someone else. Understand that for every time you have ever thought to yourself "I cannot do this", you will have to work five times harder to truly change your mind to believe that statement "I can do this" and to actually accept that the statement as the truth.

My Place, My Power, My Purpose

A midlife crisis might hit different people at different ages and perhaps the term does not apply here, but I know that eventuality of turning "The BIG 4-0" terrified me. Almost 2 years prior to the big day, I began to truly take stock of where I was in my life and started looking for answers. My search led me to question how I made choices and to focus on what needed changing in my life. My life at that time was overwhelmingly positive: I was satisfied with my relationships, I found fulfillment in my career, my health was great. The most significant area that I was truly desiring improvement was in my spiritual life. I only went to church as a child because our family went together, so my spiritual life only existed by default. Once I grew into adulthood, however, there was a disconnect, mainly because of a lack of effort on my part. Regardless of how I got there, at age 38, my desire for a satisfying spiritual life had finally become undeniable. As I did with most things I desired to learn, I ended up at the bookstore and the library on several occasions. I wasn't looking for anything from a particular religion, my interest was more practical. I began with the Bible because it was my only point of reference since childhood. I kept reading passages referring to the power of our words, both spoken and written. I found myself reading several self-improvement books at this point, but not truly finding much more than the dreaded "positive thinking" fluff and lots of reference to mantras and meditations. This felt too foreign to me and I just wasn't finding what I was looking for. I could not relate, yet there was still a connection between what I found in these books and what I knew was already in my Bible. With all of this information (both old and new) swirling around my head, I did the only thing I knew how to do – I began to pray. I prayed every morning and throughout the day the same simple prayer "Please help me understand my place, my power and my purpose in this world. Please bring me closer to You". In the weeks that followed, I began sharing my experiences with my Mother, who was eager to listen and speak from her traditional perspective. To uncover my PLACE in the world, I had to acknowledge how small I was as one person among billions, yet to realize my POWER in the world, I had to understand that even the smallest word spoken or smallest action taken by me had consequences and effects on everything around me. I always felt I had a general understanding of what my PURPOSE was in the world and it wasn't that deep. I figured my purpose was just being the best mother, wife, daughter, sister, friend, and person that I could be. But I realized that I had more to offer. My story, my knowledge and my life experiences are my legacy. It is my PURPOSE to be diligent in how I share myself in order to be a benefit of others. Most importantly, I saw the direct connection to how my words and actions had created everything I had experienced in my life so far and my thoughts, words, and actions were continuing to create what I saw and how I lived.

REALITY CHECK: YOU ARE WHAT YOU SAY YOU ARE

I'm not a big fan of having "mantras". Affirmations are closer to my comfort zone, but it's not even how I actually phrase it in my real life, because affirmations are too often associated with "fluffy, motivational words" that, too often, people either say and don't mean or they say it and don't follow up with the actions that give those "affirmations" life. I started using the term "Functional Phrases" to describe the words or phrases I used repeatedly in particular situations, or during my meditation and prayer time. As I stated before, one of the first prayers I prayed repeatedly throughout the day in an effort to improve my spiritual life was this, "Please help me understand my place, my power and my purpose in this world. Please bring me closer to You". I encourage you to start there, or with something equally simple, yet powerfully meaningful to you. Begin to create those Functional Phrases and "I Am" statements for your own life by writing them down. While it is generally true that everyone has a different learning style, I have found it to be most effective in my life when I have a Functional Phrase that I not only think, but one that it also spoken aloud often and written at least once. The combined power of bringing a phrase to life in as many ways as possible is the fast path to creating it in your life. To be clear, it is necessary for your phrases to be functional. Functional means to serve a purpose, purpose leads to an action. Begin your Functional Phrases with "I am", "I have" and "I expect". When you complete your Functional Phrases with "Now", "Today" or "In this moment", you are signaling to your brain that action must be taken on your part to make these statements true. Remember, if there is no corresponding action to the words you speak, you cannot expect anything to happen. Nothing happens until you take ACTION.

READY SET GO

Ready
What thoughts/opinions do I have regarding mantras/affirmations?

_____

_____

_____

Set
What mantras or affirmations have I tried that created zero results in my life?

_____

_____

_____

Go

What "I Am" statements can I create?

_____

_____

_____

What "I Have" statements can I create?

_____

_____

_____

What "I Expect" statements can I create?

_____

_____

_____

What actions can I take to ensure that my Functional Phrases serve a purpose in my life?

_____

_____

_____

CHAPTER TEN

TRANSFORMING IMPERFECT ENDINGS INTO NEW BEGINNINGS

EVERYONE loves a new beginning and is often filled with them: relationships, friendships, schools, jobs, children, opportunities, and homes are just a few examples of a new beginning in your life. A New Year, new look, new day, even our birthdays are markers of "the New". Despite the hopefulness that it implies, new doesn't always mean "good". There can be situations where everything may seem good at first and then the truth is surely discovered. The good news is, there is always an opportunity to remove yourself from a negative space and grow into a new positive direction. Usually, you will encounter a new beginning naturally and the excitement is genuine in those instances.

A Whole New World

There is really no way to sugar coat it: 2015 was not my year, period. As our year of turmoil began, my husband Joe and I endured the devastating impact of 3 significant deaths in the first 6 months of the year. Just days before his birthday in January, my husband's uncle died unexpectedly. A couple of months later, a very close friend of ours passed away after a brief illness. As all of this was going on, my father-in-law had been gravely ill and subsequently hospitalized for several months. The entire family and a short list of close friends made daily visits to Mount Sinai Hospital to see him. In the midst of coping with the other losses, attending to the needs of our home, parenting and being as present as possible for our children, there we were watching his father slowly slip away. I'll never forget the week that it happened. That Sunday afternoon, we had gone to the hospital as usual, yet seeing my father-in-law so frail and non-verbal that day, clearly the end was near. The drive home was uncharacteristically quiet between my husband and I. Once we made it home, I privately mentioned to Joe that I had hoped his father would be with us just a few weeks longer. I shared my fear that he wouldn't make it to the end of the week. Each day that week was a blur, just going through the motions, expecting the call that we knew was coming any day. That Thursday night we put the children to bed and fell asleep, only to be awaken by a panicked and emotional phone call from his wife at 4:00 am on that Friday morning: my husband's father was gone. As my husband rushed off to the hospital, I sat up in my darkened bedroom. The heavy weight of such an awful loss was coupled with the stark realization of my worst fear: my husband lost his father on the day of our 16th wedding anniversary. Clearly there would be no celebration, there were final arrangements being made, an obituary to write and eulogies to deliver. What followed was an intense mourning period for us both, as neither of us could shake the throes of a deep depression. At the time we both were at odds with much of his remaining relatives which left us isolated from the rest of the family and uninterested in attending any other family functions for the rest of that year. Neither my husband nor I had the strength to give each other support or encouragement, so we barely spoke to each other in the home. Once Summer rolled around, we had stopped going out altogether and we spent our evenings either completely tuned out in front of the television or fast asleep. Soon our two daughters began to notice that things were much worse than ever before, it was noticeable that were becoming affected by the overwhelmingly negative environment that our home had become. That Fall, as our children were returning to school, the black cloud that had settled over our home seemed to become permanent.

The Winter Holidays were fast approaching which meant that there would be more awkward family functions for us to avoid and since the lease on our tiny apartment was up at the end of the year, it also meant spending time looking for a new place to live, packing and moving at some point in December. I had a decision to make: I could do nothing and just continue on down the depressing Rabbit Hole ahead of me or I could stand up and choose to give our little family a chance for a fresh start and a new life. I decided that after living in Miami for 41 years, I was ready to move away for good. Our family had been to Atlanta briefly one Summer so it was definitely on the list, but honestly I had the bright lights of Las Vegas on my mind. Well, actually the suburbs on the outskirts of Las Vegas to be precise. We had been visiting friends there on a near-annual basis for over 20 years. Each time we'd visit, I would half-jokingly say to my husband that it would be a great place to live or he'd mention how easy it would be for us to move there. Without daring to give myself the time to think about it, I picked up the phone and called Joe to pop the question. I let him know that instead of renewing our lease or moving to another building near the girls' school, we could take this opportunity to pack up everything we owned and just move away to another state. I told him he just had to choose between Atlanta and Las Vegas. Through the phone, I heard Joe say the words "Las Vegas" with an excitement I had not heard in ages, it encouraged me to know that the spark of excitement still lived within him. Relieved that he was on board with the idea, I explained that by starting immediately, we could easily find a place in a new area near good schools, explain to the kids that we were moving and take our time packing and making all the necessary arrangements. I had a plan to get everything done during the kids' Winter Break from school so it would feel almost like a vacation for the kids and I worked it out with the schools in Clark County so that our children had a seamless transition from one school to the other without any absences on their records. As an added bonus, I called up my mother and asked her to come live with us in Nevada. She had recently retired, her condo was only a couple of minutes away and she was more than happy to move with us. Fortunately, she has always been a supportive influence in my life. She is an amazing grandmother to our children and she has always treated my husband more like her own son than just a son-in-law. As the 2015 drew to a close, we packed up everything we had into a U-Haul truck, paid our friend, Jeff, to make the cross-country trek with all our belongings (including our dog, Rocky) and boarded a one way flight from Miami to Las Vegas. In order to make ends meet, my husband found temporary work in nearby Los Angeles. So once we got everything settled in the new house, part of my new routine was to drive out to him every other weekend, but I didn't mind. The joy of our ultimate New Beginning made everything in 2016 beautiful again. Our daughters settled into their new school environments very well, making friends and excelling at their school work. I was able to bring my business to a completely new area and it has been very well received here. Having my mother with us has been the biggest blessing of all. She takes care of us like the amazing mother hen she has always been and most importantly, she has the space and freedom to be comfortable and truly enjoy her retirement in style. Our neighborhood is beautiful, our home is positive and filled with light and love once again. While the "Bright Lights of Las Vegas" are only visible in the distant skyline, I am still enjoying the view. Every day is still a new adventure and I am grateful that I had the courage to make great change to improve every aspect of our little family life for the better because I had the courage to make a decision to see life for all of its' possibilities.

REALITY CHECK: You're Just Getting Started

You didn't read all the way through this book just to put it down and **think** about what you can do to change your life. In fact, by this point, you have already begun to make changes to your mindset and surroundings. I know you have seen the opportunities to create the change you desire to see in your life already and now you are ready to take it to the next level. In fact, if you haven't already, take a moment and flip back through some of the notes you've written at the end of the previous chapters. See how far you've already come? Do you even remember where you were when you first began this journey? I am incredibly proud of you for all that you've accomplished thus far and I know this is only the beginning. It is time to fill an ACTUAL glass of champagne for yourself to celebrate the progress you've made and celebrate the new life you are now ready to live! Your new perspective on life will lead to many questions, these questions require answers. Once you have the answers, you must take action!

READY SET GO

Ready

How have I been holding myself back from creating positive change in my life?

_____

_____

_____

What/who have I blamed for my negative situation?

_____

_____

_____

Set

What words have I said to myself or behaviors have I displayed to truly begin to let go of the past?

_____

_____

_____

Go

What positive change will I see in my life once I focus

on my future?

_____

_____

_____

What Functional Phrases can I create to set my mind
to know that my life is set in a new positive direction?

_____

_____

_____

What positive behaviors can I begin to display to
reinforce my new, positive belief that I am heading
towards a bright, beautiful future?

_____

_____

_____

CONGRATULATIONS

Completing this book is truly only the first step in your journey. It is my desire to support you along the way. You can continue the conversation and join a community of supportive and encouraging women who are reading Imperfect 10 along with you:

www.facebook.com/groups/womensbookchat

MAXINE HABER

Made in the USA
Monee, IL
07 May 2022

95983572R00066